Yeah, Well…

Joel Landmine

Punk 💣 Hostage 💣 Press
Hollywood, California

Yeah, Well…
Joel Landmine

© Joel Landmine 2014

Punk Hostage Press
P.O. Box 1869
Hollywood, CA 90078
punkhostagepress.com

ISBN-13: 978-1-940213-93-4
ISBN-10: 1-940213-93-2

Editor: Ben Alexandre

Introduction: Joe Clifford

Cover Design & Interior Layout: SB Stokes

Bus Stop Photo: Liam O'Donnell

Ashtray Photo: Willis Stork

Tattoo Photo: Brett Reed

Editor's Acknowledgements

I would like to thank Andrew and Iris for their dedication to such an awesome cause as giving underground literature to people in prisons and institutions.

Joel Landmine is a bastard filled with stories of self-destruction and he redeems himself with brute honesty. If Johnny Cash and Jack Kerouac were to have a son, and that son chain smoked through his ugly grin, it would be Joel. He holds the esteem of everyone that matters, from his bus driver to sex workers and dive bar junkies; in short, a voice to anyone that matters. If I didn't believe in his writing I wouldn't have edited it for free. I am honored to have urinated on it several times with great joy in my heart.

Lastly, I would like to thank the Bellingham boys for their support in keeping me afloat in a sea of despair, along with Emma and Lauren. All of whom I love dearly.

But, this ain't about me... Enjoy the bullshit.

Fuck you,
Ben

Author's Acknowledgements

First and foremost I would like to thank Iris, Ben, and Razor at Punk Hostage (and SB, who has come to know this book as one knows a moody lover, the kind you love madly after only a week, and never want to see again after three) for the chance to get this thing out, to get these things read. I have been lucky enough to have some modest success doing readings around the Bay Area these last few years, but I write poems, not monologues. It seems like a lot of the work that gets done on the page gets lost on the mic. When I read I throw the pages on the floor, not to be edgy, but in the hopes that they'll get picked up and get read. This here is probably a more efficient format. I hope there's something in here that makes you feel a feeling, some kinda way.

That said, I'd like to thank all the people that gave me opportunities to read and the Bay Area writers who have supported me. John and Valerie Hirsch of The Tenderloin Reading Series *who gave me my start, Caitlin Meyer at* The Portuguese Artists Colony, *and HK Rainey and Paul Corman Roberts of* Anger Management and Revenge *(Paul was also the first to publish my work in the excellent* Full of Crow *online magazine). I've been honored to be included in a loose community of Bay Area writers that the inimitable Zarina Zabrisky has referred to as "The Beast Generation."*
The friendship and writing of her, Cassandra Dallet, William Taylor Jr., Tony DuShane, John Panzer, Charlie Getter, Joe

Clifford, Evan Karp, Bucky Sinister, SB Stokes, Youssef Alaoui, Matthew James DeCoster, MK Chavez, Tomas Moniz, and many others, have provided continuing inspiration.

I also wrote a whole list of people that have influenced my life and work, from Jimmy Santiago Baca to John Waters to Otis Redding to Bill Hicks to Raymond Carver to Hank Williams to Mississippi John Hurt to Billy Childish to Edward James Olmos and Harry Dean Stanton to...

But fuck all that. It's my father and my grandfather that I owe. So thanks, fellas. For everything.

Joel Landmine

Introduction

I hate poetry. I usually find it self- indulgent, navel-gazing, cloying pap, an archaic art form that's long out-stayed its relevance. In this brave new technological world where writing has evolved and anointed screenplay as endgame, poetry has been reduced to little more than a freakish sixth toe, as useful as an appendix.

So why am I writing the introduction to a poetry book?

Because Joel Landmine, that's why.

Since first meeting Joel, I've been mesmerized by his work. A fixture on the San Francisco literary scene for years, he's etched out a name for himself by being exactly what I wish *all* poetry *could* be.

Accessible. Relevant. Poignant and unforgettable. To quote Willy Wordsworth, Joel employs the "language really used by men." (Yes, I know about the Romantic Poets; I'm not a barbarian.)

In short, in the battle of us vs. them, Joel is one of us. (If you have to ask, you are probably one of them.) Joel writes for the butchered and abandoned, the castoff and downtrodden, and is unlike any poet I have ever read, unique in the truest sense of the word. He excels at the conversation of the lowlife, but Joel's work is steeped in the ordinary, too, infusing pop culture with philosophy, eviscerating the minutia and mundane that sometimes yields a world of riches. At least to those of us who have nothing.

Squalor paints his scene, dejection his theme—but it's love, however fleeting, bizarre, unholy, perverted or downright religious (in the strictest unorganized sense) that remedies. There is a burning love and passion that colors this work, the desire of one man to reach out in the dark and confusion to say, "Hey, baby, I'm just as fucked up as you. Let's have a smoke and compare tattoos. Then maybe later, we can get naked. Here, let me light that for you."

Now *that's* the kind of poetry I want to read.

Joe Clifford

For Nathan

Table of Contents

"God knows I tried. I tried hard to be right."
                    -Junior Kimbrough

"I tried. I tried to do the best I could, but sometimes I guess my best ain't good."
                    -The Geto Boys

"Finally, we begin to see that all people, including ourselves, are to some extent emotionally ill as well as frequently wrong."
                    -Anonymous

"Fuck 'em."
                    -E-40

Prologue:
I wrote a letter to a lover, and broke in to her apartment with my old key to leave it on her bed, which was over the line, I know, but at least I didn't take the bus across town to punch her stupid fucking boyfriend in the throat like I wanted to

It went like
this:

Dear Dollface,
      Fuck you.
Love,
      Joel

What can I say?

I'm a poet.

John Law May Or May Not Have Beaten My Ass, But I Will Never Ever Know Because I'm A Wino And I Fall Down A Lot

Getting out of jail is a lot like
walking out of a movie theater
into daylight. Your whole body
squints
like those pinky mice they sell
at the pet store to
feed to snakes.

(I vaguely remember that)
They kicked me out of the makeshift detox
for street drunks
(ten mattresses covered in plastic and a
blood pressure machine
in an abandoned office lobby downtown)
at six in the morning

I went down to Sixth Street with enough
hustle left
in me to get enough cheap whiskey
in me to come to
in jail at ten a.m.

I woke up behind glass
as though someone had put a zoo
exhibition in a modern office.
The other side was all cubicles,
tiny desks with computers and in/out boxes
piled high.

My side was barren, not even a bench.
The smooth cement floor gently sloped
toward
a drain in the center of the cell,
I guess so they could hose me down easily
if need be.

The only decoration was a small tile
partition,
barely concealing the toilet,
that futuristic primitive toilet,
all stainless steel,
no seat.

That toilet became well acquainted with
both ends of me that day.
We spent the day together.

Otherwise I tried to sleep on that floor.

That floor that taught me the meaning of
cold and

                                     hard,

and I am a man who has slept in alleys,
under tables in bars to be swept up at closing
                                     time,
once sitting up in a plastic chair at a shelter
because they were out of mats.

My body was bruised over every inch.
When I fall down drunk,
I usually break my fall with my face.
My face was fine,
so it probably wasn't that.

★★★

I didn't know the part of town near the
jailhouse.
After four hours of wandering the streets
I found myself
at the fucking McDonald's right
next to the jail.
I could have sworn I heard laughing.
I called my mother collect,
she cried and cried,

said she couldn't help me out,
she just couldn't.

I would have called Babygirl,
but she'd long since stopped picking up the phone.

★★★

I somehow hitched a ride.
Ten hours and thirty miles
later, I got to my father's
house.
He was on vacation.
I broke in through a kitchen window,
smoked some weed I'd
hidden in an old suit in the hall closet.
I got in to bed
and curled myself around a liter of scotch
that,
at that point,
was worth more than I was.

It was the most comfortable fucking bed I'd
ever been in.
More comfortable even than all those plush
beds

of all those sweet pretty women,
to whom I'd left nothing to remember me by
but the fresh tattoo ink
I'd sweated on their fancy sheets.

A Christmas Miracle

Yesterday was Christmas.
A tiger escaped from
its home at the zoo
and ate a guy.

Really.

It mauled
two more.
The newspaper
said that it had not walked through

the only door
to its enclosure. There was
also
a 15 foot moat and a twenty foot
wall.

The tiger could not, the paper went on,
jump that great a distance. So nobody
knows, the paper
says,
how it got out,
its escape

a mystery.

Poem About Breaking and Entering #2

"Thank you so much for letting me
stay, Nathan. I had nowhere
else to go."

"What are you talking about? What
are you *doing* here?

I told you three times at the bar
that you COULDN'T stay! I didn't
even know you were here!"

I felt myself wilt like a time lapse film of
flowers in fall.

"How did you even get *in* here?!" he said.

Poem About Breaking and Entering #7

I woke up on an overstuffed black leather
couch,
feeling like the last third of a 40 oz. tastes,
in an apartment I didn't recognize.

An old man in a silk bathrobe was
yelling at me.

"Who ARE you?!
What are you DOING here?!"
His face was turning red,
a vein bulged on his forehead.

His wife stood slightly behind him to the left.
She was dressed, lavishly, tastefully.
She had a silk scarf
fastened with a brooch from Tiffany's
or someplace.
These were clearly rich people. Everything
was

spotless, perfectly placed, looked expensive.
        They
                probably
had an interior decorator.

Her face was calm, kind.
"HOW DID YOU GET IN HERE?!" he
screamed.
Sitting up now, I gulped for air like a
goldfish.

"You don't know, do you dear?" she said
calmly.

"No ma'am I don't thank you so much for
your hospitality!" I blurted and bolted

for the door. I was all the way down the hall
in
three
improbable strides.

I had to chuckle to myself as I stopped,
walked slowly back, and knocked politely
three times on their door.

I had forgotten my shoes.

An Errand

We were going to her family's house for
                                   dinner,
I think it was her Mother's birthday.

I had gotten her daughter ready, made sure
her hair was brushed,
gotten her into her jacket,
gotten her into the car seat.

As we drove across town toward the
freeway
north,
she pulled to the curb in front of the bar.

I looked at her blankly,
uncomprehending.

She looked at me hard and just said,
"We're already late, hurry up."

I ran inside,
the door closing behind me a tiny, rapid
dusk,

told the bartender "We're going to her
Mother's. Let me have a shot."

He smiled, filled a tumbler to the rim.
I took it back in one swallow,
left a dollar on the bar, and trotted back out
to the car.

As she pulled back out into the autumn
                              afternoon sunlight,
Sadie in her car seat singing softly along
with the radio,
we didn't say a word, but I knew

then

that she loved me like she said
she did.

A Little Piece

Nine months sober.
I live in a halfway house.
I have no job.
More than a year
ago I lost everything in
the world
that I gave a fuck about.

A woman.
A child.
A job.

A home.

Solace.

A cat.

The halfway house
where I live has
a cat.

Over the years
with all the comings

and goings
he has grown docile.

Sometimes,
when he's around
and I'm around

I bring him to my
room
and lie down on
my bed.
He lays nearby.

Sometimes
he purrs.

And I finally get

some peace.

Poem Fragment About The Wind #1

The wind
turns
my ancient window
into an angry
drunk in the back of
a squad car,

violently
thrashing in vain, against

the shackles of
its frame.

Chicharrones

She came by on a Friday night.
We both played it cool,
pretended there was nothing strange about it.
Her new fella didn't like movies,
she wanted to see this old flick with Warren Oates
and Harry Dean Stanton,
and I had it.

I had gone out to the store,
bought her the root beer
and gummy raspberry candies
she likes,
picked up the room a little,
emptied the ashtrays.

She wouldn't kiss me back.

"I've missed you, estúpida," I said.
"Then you shouldn't have dumped me, fool."
I had nothing to say.
She let me kiss her all over,
rest my hand on her leg,
grip her arm like I had
sometimes liked to do,

but she wouldn't kiss me back.

She lay on her stomach
texting him. Her
short skirt rode up,
I looked at those tattooed thighs
I liked so much,
that glorious line where
they met her little brown ass,
her crimson panties where
they came together.

I touched her thighs idly as she texted away,
that phone that seemed an extension of
her hand,
smiled to myself at her gold toenail polish.
I slid those red panties aside,
slid them off,
quietly ate her pussy.
She waited until she came before becoming indignant.

We watched, we talked, it got late.

She wouldn't kiss me back.

God bless her,
she stuck to her guns.
I had to admire that.

She told me she was tired,
took off her clothes,
got beneath the covers.

I turned off the lights,
put a Richard Conte movie on low,
and held her close, the way she likes,
until she fell asleep.

When her breathing got heavy,
I kissed her forehead and whispered to her.
"I'm sorry, Chicharron. I'm so, so
sorry."

★★★

I don't know if you've ever spent a night
like that
with someone you ain't supposed to.
Nights like that live outside of time,
in some sweet limbo,
and in the morning there's a savory anxiety,
the knowledge that once one of you gets up and leaves,

the spell is broken. Reality rushes in,
like water into a submarine with broken portals.
Pumpkin time.

We cuddled in bed, the quiet morning
light filtered through
my dirty windows.

"I love you," she said out loud,
for the first time ever,
perhaps still thinking me half asleep,
her voice betraying the resentment and affection
she'd been so careful to hide.
I looked into her face,

said "Pardon me?"
"I won't repeat it," she whispered, looking down.
I wrapped her in my arms,
held her face to my chest,
whispered back.
I'd often told her I loved her,
just never when she was awake.

We fucked that morning,
twice, trying to grip that last few hours,
draw it out.

I savored the way her tooth caught on her lip,
like it always does.
Still,
she wouldn't kiss me back.

She kept looking at her phone, though.
That fucking phone.
I got real quiet.
"WHAT?" she asked in that sexy,
bratty way that she does.

"Maybe I just saw your phone," I said,
"Maybe it was a picture of you and dude.
Maybe I got real fucking jealous," I said.
"Maybe that's irrational," I said.
"Maybe I don't fucking care," I said.

"That's not my fault," she shot back matter-of-factly,
and went back to whatever it was that she was doing.

I scowled, pouted tough,
but I knew that she was right.
Finally the time came,
we got up,

got dressed.
But before we walked out to the street together,
before our tone changed,
before our conversation became louder,
superficially nonchalant,

we stood by the door,
I drew her to me,
one arm hard around her waist,
the other hand on her face,
I kissed her hard on her mouth.

And she kissed me back, just the once.

Bobby Says To Say Hello

The light,
that
comforting, sickly
yellow
of lit rooms in old photographs,
the small worn table, square,
against
one wall.

This cozy apartment kitchen
a beating man's heart
in the giant's corpse of this labyrinth
mansion.

Your Father and I
sit with chipped mugs
and talk frankly of you,
old friends,
though we have never met.

★★★

Odd, long dead, he visits only *my*
dreams.
This always makes you angry,

as if I've somehow
summoned him
willfully, out of some
vague spite.

Of course
I haven't.
Just one more bullet
for the assault

rifle of your jealousy,
whose barrel never cools.

I Am Proud To Be An American

Ain't nobody ever
     got their heart broke

that didn't fall in
     love with something first.

I Saw You On The Bus Downtown Again
Today (Hello Stranger)

With apologies to Barbara Lewis

I moved across a bay
to escape
your memory.

But the last time
I climbed onto
a bus downtown,
it was the most
crowded
bus
I'd ever been on,
people pushing and shifting,

tidal,

like the front row of the Danzig show
we went to
that time you lost your skirt,

or cattle on a train.

I looked up, and there you were,

(Hello Stranger)
holding Addy,
both of you smiling down
at me from
just above all of our heads,
nestled
between an ad for a
personal injury lawyer
and another
for
City College.

Both of you
smiling down on me,
(Sh-bop sh-bop my baby)
like a spotlight
just
on
me,
(Sh-bop sh-bop my baby oooh)
even in
the late afternoon
sun,

taking me from
there,

all the way back home.

But no,
just a photo.

This ain't no fucking metaphor,
it wasn't a woman that looked like you,
it was a picture of *you*.
(Seems so good to see you back again,)
Stock photography,
taken from way back then
(how long has it been? A-ooh)
and put on this city bus,
a spot for
women's services.

"I never hit her,"
I wanted to say, to explain,
(It seems like a mighty long time)
"I wouldn't!"
But, of course,
they couldn't know,
wouldn't care.
Just some woman

and a little girl
in an ad on the bus.

***

(Oh my my my,
sh-bop, sh-bop my baby)

***

I had almost
forgotten about it until
today. I got on
the bus, downtown
again.

I looked up,
expecting to
see you there
and
(seems like a mighty long time)
sure enough,
there was

your
face,
(I'm so glad
you stopped to say hello to me,)
your faces, smiling down
on me.

(remember that's the way it used to be? ah–ooh)

★★★

You told me
you'd like to see it sometime
(Sh-bop sh-bop, my baby oooh).

Well meet me
downtown, Babygirl.

We'll ride the bus.

Bus Girlfriends

I.

Thighs on the train in
the Sunday afternoon light,

obstructed from my view and revealed again,
as people get on and off
like the
setting and rising of the sun,
a hundred little mornings.

She stepped off at her stop,
(To go home to her lonely apartment?
To a pair of loving arms?
To finish her run?)
those thighs that
give shorts a reason to live.

In her stead
two Latin couples
that didn't know each other,

the men holding their rucas close.

II.

I see you around town sometimes
and when I look at your face

I know I could fall in love with you.
I kind of fucking hate you for that.

III.

Little goth girl,
all fishnet and gangly arms,
and those impossibly perfect tits that are
wasted on young girls,
giant kitten eyes peering out from her makeup,
the tattoo on her chest as cute, and standard,
and shy as her
pretty frightened face.

Her platform boots
might fool the boys in the club,
but here, on the train,
they looked awkward and ridiculous.
I guess that's always been true of girls like that.

She gave me a look as I chuckled out loud to
myself for thinking
"If only I were ten years younger,"
and then
"O Lord, O Lord, it's already come to this."

When we got off at the same stop,
she looked worried and hopeful

that maybe
I was following her.

★★★

A few days later I saw a woman on the street.
She looked to be in her sixties,
her tiny leopard print mini-dress
showing off to the world her expensive tan.

She wore chunky, gaudy jewelry and sunglasses,
and had short cropped bleached hair,
like a character from a John Waters movie
about the mafia.

As I got closer I saw that she was chatting
with the jailbait goth girl.

I saw her recognize me from the train,
and she about jumped out of her skin
as I winked while I strolled past.

Fortune Cookie Fortune About Social Stratification, Institutional Racism, and The American Criminal Justice System

The man with holes in his shoes must be extra careful not to step in shit.

A Reminder

A stranger's notes
in a

book from the library.

I think they
were
looking for inspiration.

Any Old Piece Of Shit

My boy won't talk to me;
this is nothing new, he hasn't for years.
His mother calls, says his wife has left him,
that he has money trouble,
ulcers,
drinks too much,
moved to Montana or some God damned place…
Chip off the old block.

I put the phone back in its cradle,
pour myself a drink.

The days blur together;
this is nothing new, they have for years.
I work so much that all my T-shirts are
                              utility orange,
no reason to buy the other ones.
I see bubble levels in my sleep,
work gloves, needle nosed pliers.
Hamburger helper has no idea what a
                    help he is, man.

Every night with a glass in one hand,
God damned spatula in the other,
poised over the pan like a claw hammer.

The boys at the video store are always glad
                              to see me;
This is nothing new, they've been there for
                                    years.
They smile, they call me "Jimmy."
Best part of my day.

I bring them my old records sometimes,
and God bless 'em,
they still light up.

It's science fiction these days,
any old piece of shit.
The drinks are still good,
and when I get home,
sit in my chair,
press play,
and take that first long draw...

I lied. This is the best part of my day.
I don't pretend to have this old world
figured out,
but what do I really need that I ain't got?
I figure that makes me pretty God damned
lucky...

Poem Fragment About The Wind #2

Force without intent,
                    the wind
                        begs
            plaintively, insistently, hungrily

                    for...
                                    What?

Crusader's Lament

It is a woeful mistake
to want one thing in this world
more than all other things.

With enough ambition,
or rotten fucking luck,
one day you might get it.

Then what?

I Say Oh My and A Boo Hoo

I learned to fuck from listening to
Stooges records.

When it's good, it's visceral, a little bit violent,
a kind of intimate brutality.

As we lay on the mattress on the floor of my
little bedroom off the garage she
waved my smoke away and said
"Sometimes when we fuck you slap my face.
When you're doing that, what are you thinking about?"

The implication seemed to be that some
deep misogyny, or psychological force, or
malice was at work. How could I explain
that fucking is the only time
there *is* no thinking?

It's primitive, primal,
strictly wolfman time. When it's over I'm
back to Larry Talbot,
self-conscious, baffled, neurotic.

Once I start thinking, it's fucking over.

Thinking is DEATH to fucking.

What does a mongoose think about
as it kills a cobra?

"Does it bother you?" I asked.

"Fuck no," she said.

Vagrant Stump Speech, Turk & Leavenworth, 2012 (Lord Help the Poor & Needy)

He said
He didn't know how to drive!
He didn't even know how to read!
He didn't know how to boil an egg!
Kruschev didn't even know how to make oatmeal!
That's how Kennedy felt about Kruschev,
every American knows how to boil an egg!
Every American knows how to make oatmeal!

In 1963 Kennedy was talking loudly!
Talking loudly in German!
That's why Johnson invented noise cancelling headphones!
Noise cancelling headphones!

Maybe he was just crazy,
but he sounded like he knew what
he was talking about.

I can drive a stick,
I can read and make oatmeal, and I know more
than one person that I wish
would shut the fuck up. But

maybe I need to
make a scene every once in a while.

Or maybe

I just need to learn
how to boil an egg.

A Shameful Victory

I fucking hate pigeons.
They're like rats, but without the ingenuity.

I emerged
from one of those scaffolding mineshafts
to see one pecking at trash
just off the curb.

I spit at it,
nailed it on the back directly between
its wings,
a full-on thick smoker's hack gob,
all mucous, heavy.

It bobbed
its idiot head wildly,
tried to touch its wings together behind its back,
spun around in circles there in the gutter.

My lips
peeled back into one of those uncontainable
grins, my teeth bared,
my satisfaction palpable.

I looked
up and, there across the street,
an old woman was stopped dead in her
tracks, aghast, had seen the whole
transaction.

She gave
me one of the dirtiest looks
that any person has ever given me.

★★★

Moments earlier
we'd all been alone.
But now here we were

sharing a moment
together in the street,

the three of us.

Determination

My father
told me a story once, about
a man he knew

whose wife had
gone blind. She
said she'd bought some eye drops
that were tainted

with lye. They began
(this man and his
blind wife)
legal proceedings against

the eye drop
company.

But

when the doctors
examined her eyes, they
found no evidence
of the kind

of damage that

lye might cause.
As a matter of fact, they
found nothing

the matter with
her *eyes* at all...

★★★

It came out,
then,
that the woman was
crazy.

She had made it
all up.
Except that she
was, indeed,

as blind as if God
Himself had
swallowed The Heavens
and
The Earth.

★★★

She had simply
stared into the sun
until
everything disappeared

to a single point,
like a picture tube on an
old television
finally burning out.

And then,

not even that...

Unfocused Poem
About Astral Projection

The 3AM fog is
that palpable mist of 1940s werewolf movies,
when streetlights become
little pale suns,
coronas like swarms of gnats.
When the chill makes
the parked cars and thin apartment windows
look like lazy men
sweating in the heat.

Feeling sweet and calm and sad
I look at the nearly full moon,
aural, like the streetlamps,
at once majestic and pathetic,
alone, obese.
I wonder whether it's shining
through your window,
through that gauzy orange curtain of yours.

I stare and stare at it
through the window of the cab
all the way down Guerrero,

but I am somehow also there with you,
your head on my chest,
my eyes squinting at my book in the semidarkness,
listening quietly to
your sleeping breath.

Stepping out of the cab,
I stop.
The gutter is filled with petals,
pink carnation petals,
spilling into the storm drain.
I try to take a picture,
but my batteries have died.

I can see our whole lives together,
stretching toward some imaginary future,
as the desert highway stretches
to the horizon.

I struggle to understand how,
having known you so briefly,
I can so certainly and simply love you,
can so calmly accept your loss.

I'm full of wonder, I
suppose…

shit.

Justice

I found pamphlets
advertising feng shui
scattered
all over the staircase.

Feedback

A reviewer
once described my poems as

"abrupt."

A Win, A Loss

He said,
"It's region
two.
Do you have an all-region DVD player?"

"Naw man.

I won my DVD player playing
bingo
at a halfway house
on New Year's Eve.
It

doesn't even
have a remote."

All Her Tiny Black Sneakers

I stayed up
all night
busting my ass to get it
perfectly,
gloriously wrong again.
So while I was batting zero...

We walked.

I told her, spilled it, let fly...

that when
we walk, or sit, or embrace,
I feel like I'm home
and I feel
so
so
nervous.

So nervous.

I didn't tell her how the soft give of her hip,
all them tiny black sneakers,
had filled my thoughts,
popping corn in hot oil,

locust swarms.

"What is THAT
 like?" she asked.

"Kind of tickles,"
I shrugged.

I also left out
the part where she
had made me feel feelings
that I'd forgotten I
had, and that THAT
scared me out of my fucking mind.

And then,
like a fool,
I didn't kiss her.

I can wait.

On The Large Portrait of Child Murderer Albert Fish Hanging In My Living Room

Old man, brown three piece suit, seated.
I tell the nice folks that come over sometimes
that it's Sigmund Freud in the portrait.
Nobody ever questions this,
though Freud had a full beard.

His hand to his forehead, as though repentant—
this is artistic license. Fish went to
the electric chair laughing,
shorted the first one out with the
29 sewing needles lodged in the flesh
between his balls and his asshole,
laughed at his executioners even then,
the sick fuck.

You can't see these in the portrait, of course,
the needles,
but I've seen the X-rays.

He was finally caught when he wrote
a long letter to
the parents of one of his victims

detailing the horrible death of their child.
There is glee in that letter,
and I feel like a worse person just for having read it.

It's so rare that,
deep down,
evil comes this fucking...

unsympathetic.

The Beadle Family Murder of 1782

"It truly gives me pain for to pen down,
a deed so black, and yet his mind was sound.
Says he, 'I mean to close six persons' eyes,
through perfect fondness and the tend' rest ties'"

-Traditional

A reader to the end,
William Beadle, his business failing,
found solace
not in the bottom of a bottle, but between the
                                                bindings.

A reader to the end,
he concluded in his scholarly pursuits,
as so many men have,
that there is no earthly gain to be had, except
interminable misery.

As a caring husband and father,
and a reader to the end,
he sought freedom from the inescapable
                                                bondage of

suffering offered by This World.
For his wife and children he sought only freedom.

He drugged them one night before bed.
When they had all drifted off,
a reader to the end,
he calmly laid down his book and picked up
                                        his knife.
When the gingham sheets were soaked,
his family's liberty assured,

he breathed a sigh of relief, and,
(a reader to the end)
uttered to himself
"In the land of the blind,
the one eyed man is king,"

then shot himself in the face.

He thought, perhaps,
a reader to the end,
that they would be reborn,
the mythical phoenix rising from the flames,

and not just shitbirds charred in a drifter's bonfire.

A reader to the end.
I wonder what he was reading.

Suspension

29 years old
at a (barely) converted industrial
warehouse in Oakland, CA.
(perversely called The Oakland
Metropolitan Opera House),
in darkness except for the lights from the stage
(that ornately hung galaxy in the ceiling),

in a rented bunny suit (really),
I sit in a rickety, unfinished wooden chair,
somehow feeling less
ridiculous than all these other
grown people
in their shiny black
and elaborate eyeliner.

On the cabaret table in front of me
sits a plastic bag
filled with organic carrot rinds,
(tomorrow I will shit carrot-orange)
as the ashtray on my desk at home is
filled with cigarette butts.

★★★

The woman I intended to marry
got married this past weekend.
She's pregnant again.

The woman I love is…
God knows where,
can't be bothered
(And who can blame her?).

The woman with whom things are currently
imploding is hanging
(quite literally) from hooks through
her back and knees
on the stage in front of me.

How
(O *how*)
did I get…

The Gay Divorcee

I passed a car
on the freeway
with streamers and stuff hanging off…

and the words "just divorced"
written in soap
on the rear windshield.

Nuclear Envelope

Lately
the invisible gaps in my life
have been making their presence known,

the way
the gaps between your teeth
announce their presence after a cleaning.

Proximity and distance have become
improbably disparate
again.

Again.

★★★

I keep having this dream.
In the dream I can fly,
which you would think would be pretty cool.

Problem is,
I can't land.

I can get my feet within millimeters of the ground,
but they never quite touch,

I can slow down,
but I can never quite stop,

can't stand still,
can never sit down.

Green Grass

As my life fills
back up,
I grow nostalgic
for the recent past
when it was...

emptier.

Meanwhile, At The Existential Laundromat

What is it about the lint trap
that so captures my imagination?

Reading Series

For Paul Corman-Roberts

Sitting in a dark café
sipping espresso,
and underlining passages in a book by a
French philosopher and historian,
about to get up for a poetry reading,

I felt so pathetically, revoltingly *bohemian,*
so very fucking precious,
that I wanted to
drag myself out to the alley,

and beat my own ass.

Fury, and Its Negative Correlation With Eloquence

Minding my own business, waiting
for the bus to my classes at the University,
an old man with long grey hair and
an expensive road bike,

resplendent in his neon lycra
biking togs,
took it upon himself to
aggressively bust my balls

for smoking at the bus stop.

He spoke with righteous indignation, as
though he were speaking as a
spokesman of the community.
At least I think that was his intention. But
from where I stood, he came at me

as though I were drinking from the wrong
drinking fountain.

My hand moved instinctively
to the folding knife

in my pocket,
and I wanted to say

"If it means one less entitled fucking
gabacho that thinks it's the world's
responsibility to ensure *his* personal comfort
at all times, then I hope this is the cigarette
that gives you fucking *cancer*.
Myself, I find saggin'-ass old white men in
spandex objectionable. But *I* took my
fucking chances when I left the fucking
house this morning.
You're in fucking *Oakland*, punk! Go back
to Berkeley with that *shit*."

But I didn't say that.

Not because I thought the better of it and
held my tongue.
I'm no spiritual giant,
and believe we had words, him and me,

but rather
because I didn't think of it until five
minutes later,
sitting on the bus

seething
with impotent rage.

Mean Streets

"It's a little embarrassing," I said, "but I
write poetry.
I'm doing a reading next week.
You should come by if you can."

"What do you write about?" she asked.

"Story poems, mostly," I replied, "They
don't rhyme or anything."
I shifted my weight from
foot to foot,
embarrassed.

She was kind of a salty broad,
but I mean she was sitting in a café,
reading a book,
an actual book, not one of those
computerized gizmos.

She was a salty broad,
I knew her from the AA meetings
we both attended,
but she drank loose leaf herbal tea, for
Christ's sake...

"But what are they *about?*" she insisted.
"Life on the *mean streets?*"
She was a salty broad.

Her sarcasm stung, but I laughed it off.

"Um, sort of.
I mean, I don't think anybody wants to read
about
me lying in bed watching movies and
snuggling with my cat."

"You never know," she said, adjusting
her glasses
and looking back down at her book, dismissing me.
"*I* might."

I went home,
put on *The King of Comedy*,
and as Rudy licked his paws,
I thought about what she had said.

I Don't Get To Touch You Anymore

The skin on her
belly, her hips,
porous, pebbled.
Not pillow soft,
not feather soft,
not fur soft.

Soft like treated
leather, calfskin,
like river rocks,
give like the legs
on a fat baby.

I make sure to fill
the water glass
that lives on the nightstand,
should she awake
thirsty (as she
often does), like a child,
in the night.

**She Would Spend Hours Getting Ready,
Trying On Five or Six Outfits, Getting Her
Hair And Makeup Just Right When We Used
To Just Meet Up For Coffee Once Or Twice
A Week, But I Never Loved Her More Than
When She Came Fresh From The Shower,
Unadorned, Sleepy, and Ready For Bed**

Longing is a useless, girlish
emotion
that I'd like very much
to be rid of.

I Know, I Know. It's Serious.

For Moz, Eli Lilly & Co., and
William Taylor Jr.

It was a deep depression.

It had been going on for months.
It started with a chick who didn't feel the
way I thought she ought to,
and then fed on itself,
festering,
as these things do.

I was wearing out the grooves on all my
honky-tonk records,
my blues records,
the kitchen floor covered in bottles,
I was filthy,
wasn't eating.
I was having trouble getting to work,
and I didn't work until four in the afternoon.
It was getting ridiculous.

I was working with my best friend that night.
I went and pulled the Morrissey tape off the shelf,
put it with the employee holds.

He saw the tape and he panicked.
"You're *depressed*!" he shouted when he'd
finished with his customer,
"You can't watch *MORRISSEY VIDEOS*!
You'll fucking *kill yourself*!"

"You don't understand," I said,
"I fucking hate Morrissey.

Here's what's gonna happen:
I'm gonna go home,
get good and drunk,
watch the goddam tape,
take a good look at Morrissey,
and I will be so ashamed and embarrassed
that I've been taking myself so fucking seriously,
that this will all be over."

And that is exactly what I did.

Lock Groove

The same thoughts
rattle
around my head,
(skull?)
like the shuttle
in a can of Krylon,
the widget
in a
pint can of stout.
Or,

more accurately,

like a marble
in a mason jar.

For Better Or For Worse, Being A Man In A Patriarchal Society Means That I Can Pee Pretty Much Wherever The Fuck I Want

In the Vietnamese noodle place
by the lake

there is
a unisex restroom

and a men's room.

Traitors

Lately he's been crying without weeping,
the tears like ants,
or Kamikaze pilots,
giving their lives for the greater good.

They appear suddenly,
from nowhere,
drunken drivers around blind turns.
At work by the sign that said "Open Trench"
on Church and Dubose,
buying a danger dog from those street
vendors down on Mission street,
when he's riding the bus.

Never sobs,
just tears.

It began to happen more and more,
it was embarrassing.
He tried eye drops,
even saw an optometrist.

But still they came,
always surprising him like landmines,
betraying a past
he could never quite remember.

Riviera

There are those that want a Lotus or a
Bentley.
And some folks want an Escalade with
twenty two inch Daytons.

Some kind souls just want to drive one of
them hybrid cars that
get real quiet when
you drive 'em slow.

Some folks even ask for Jesus to help them
get that van or pickup,
and hell,
from the stories I've heard,
sometimes He even does.

Me, all I ever wanted was a 1964 Buick
Riviera.
The lines, the power, those signature scoops
on the side.
Like driving a shark. A loud, steel shark.

I found one once,
a beautiful gunmetal grey,
all that chrome,

whitewall tires.
Just right for me,
it had even been outfitted with a tape deck.
But once I'd bought it there were…

problems.

The belts were worn,
the transmission slipped
and bucked.
Even the windshield wipers
would turn off or on without warning,
unpredictably,
as though possessed.

Driving it became scary,
but not in the exhilarating way.
Its unpredictability, its unreliability,
became irritating, wearisome,
finally outright exhausting.

I doted on it so,
but I became resentful,
there was only so much I could do.

I'm not a mechanic.
I don't have the time or inclination to learn.
Wading through a junkyard looking for parts
sounds romantic,
but let's be honest.
I have shit to do.

★★★

So I sold it.
The guy who bought it was
a friend of a friend.

I would see him driving it around the city,
and would be seized with jealousy,
blind rage.

He looked so *cool*!
In *my* fucking car!
I wanted to kill him,
would see it parked
and want to key it,
slash his tires,
put sugar in the gas tank.

I had only myself to blame,
had given it up,

glad to be rid of it.
But this irrational *rage*!
It was *mine*, and I wanted it *back*!

★★★

But then something happened.
I was riding the bus in the rain,
and saw him standing by the side of the road,
the hood smoking,
waiting for triple-A.
It happened once,
twice,
three times.

I laughed and laughed
at his misfortune,
so glad
that it was *his* problem now.

★★★

And, Baby,
that's what happened with you and me.

The Prophet

Intrepid and misguided explorer Stanley
Livingstone
set out down the Nile in 1866,
to explore Darkest Africa.
And that he did.

His assistants deserted him one by one,
and though deathly ill,
having been robbed of his supplies,
medicine and rations,
he struggled ever southward,
completely losing
contact with the outside world
for six long years.

As a teenager
I undertook a safer and briefer,
though similarly ill advised, expedition.
I did it by taking psilocybin mushrooms,
in my bedroom,
alone,
at night,
as often as I could afford.

★★★

I used to buy them by the trash–filled lagoon
behind my high school,
(where we smoked cigarettes and bammer weed,
and hash when we could get it,
on our lunch breaks,
ever watchful for Levi,

the bicycle riding security guard)
from a character named Wayne who
fascinated and frightened me,
though in retrospect he too
was just a boy.

Wayne looked like the snake
in the 1973 Walt Disney film version of
Robin Hood,
but with acne and a long, oily Kurt Cobain
haircut.
He used to carry tabs of acid in the frayed
cuffs
of his tattered hoodie.

He became a legend
when he went on the run from
some hallucinated enemy,
in the stolen car of a friend's parent,

and nearly made it to Washington state
before he was arrested,

(in our imaginations) smiling and snarling for
the terrified newspaper cameras
like Charles Starkweather.

Anyway,
on one such night,
I ventured out of the safe cave of
my bedroom,
down the hallway,
like Livingstone down The Nile,
to get something from the kitchen.

★★★

Once there,
I bumped into my father,
an engineer and physician,
whose educated opinion I trust and respect.

We regarded each other warily,
since we both knew the other should be fast
asleep,
but, though I was tripping balls
and his face wouldn't stay

still,
we engaged in some friendly chit-chat.

And then,
apropos of nothing,
he paused, looked at me,
and said

"Son…
You're just not very good at *life*."

After what was probably a very brief
(but seemed like a very long)
pause I replied,

"Dad, that's a little broad for me tonight.
Perhaps we could discuss it another time."

And I began my trek back up The Nile.
Though that other time
has never come,
　　　　　I haven't forgotten our discussion.

Tiffany's

I went into the Tiffany's
on Union Square with
     my father.

It was crowded,
Neil Young was the only other
shabby-looking motherfucker in the joint.
I was clearly the only one without money
     to burn.

We went upstairs.
The girl behind the counter
looked at the rings through my ears,
at the heavy ring
     hanging from my nose.

"You look like you're good on jewelry," she
said,
     and laughed nervously.

I looked her up and down,
     looked her right in her eye.

"What can you show me
     in stainless steel?"

Too $hort and Biggie Study Body Fat Deposition For Midterm On The Evolution of Human Sexual Dimorphism

10–20% of lady fat
is called Gluteofemoral Fat
that they store during childhood and puberty
It has extra nutrients for when they
produce milk

I thought I'd never remember the word
"Gluteofemoral"

until this morning
when I realized it just mean "ass and thighs"
in Latin

All we want is hoes
Gluteofemoral hoes

Why Would You Do That?

Sick in bed,
I dreamed that you showed up at my house.
You were laughing as
you woke me up
by rubbing your bare feet
on my face.

At first I was mad
that you would
come all that way
just to
do something like that
to me.

Then I was even madder
when I realized
you hadn't.

Phantom Limb Syndrome

The poems pour out
like dry heaves, like
scraping the last
meat
of melon from the
rind.

But there's hurt

I just can't
get at,
worms in wood,
rats in the walls,

the skin of a kernel
of popping corn
trapped between the teeth and gums,
cutting ever deeper
and always

just

out of reach.

She Drinks Her Water Room Temperature

On the 26 city bus, late for school, but
relaxed,
satisfied (so rare),
I stopped reading for a second,
and smiled, squinting,
into the sunlight.
I could still
smell your pussy on my upper lip,
canary feathers in my cats' grin.

Soft and clear in my mind,
bathed in the morning light that
filters through the thin cloth over your
bedroom window,
I could see your face.
Just this morning

and just fifteen years old,
all that time ago.

Another Cliché Poem
About A Cure For Writer's Block

For straight men and lesbians. I bet the rest
of you will probably know what I'm talking
about too.

It's easy.
Just fall in love with a triflin'-ass ho.

I mean really get it bad for a woman that can
really ruin your life.

I'm talkin' that compulsive,
long-gone-lonesome-blues, by-the-time-I-
get-to-Phoenix,
ain't-too-proud-to-beg kind of love.

I'm talkin' the kind of love
where you get 72-hour-hold panic attacks
when you can't be with her,
and you're so lonely that you want to die
when you are.

Love like trying to hold on to a fistful of
boiling water.

Love like a year old meth habit.

It's like they say.

A smooth sea
don't make for no skilled sailor.

Epilogue:

Untitled Poem About An Old, Tired Story That Precludes A Happy Ending

My best friend
hooked me up
with a close girlfriend of hers.

She was exquisite, this friend.
Long hair,
tattooed head to toe,
a talented artist herself.

She was gorgeous,
big, sad eyes
and a fine, odd sense of humor.

We had an immediate rapport,
our affair
burned
bright and hot,
and we were soon a couple.

But

it soon (too soon)
became apparent that
there was a mess inside her,
a mess I hadn't made
and couldn't clean up.

★★★

Come Christmas Eve
I was driving down the coast in my
roommate's car to see my mother.

I stopped at a strip mall in a dying old surf
town
to buy my momma a present.

She was fond of napping,
my mother,
so I went in to a
discount department store to
get her a plush leopard-print
throw pillow.

As I waited in line,
my phone buzzed in my pocket.

A text from my girlfriend:

"I miss you."

I put my phone back in my pocket,
and rolled my eyes.
I felt a twinge of sadness at my callousness,
this odd private moment out in public.

★★★

I put the pillow in the car,
and walked across the parking lot
to get a cup of coffee.

As I waited in line,
my phone buzzed in my pocket.

A text from my best friend:

"I miss you."

I put my phone back in my pocket,
and my heart burst right the fuck out my
chest.
Butterflies, the whole bit.

It hit me like a cancer diagnosis
left on an answering machine.

Fuck *me*.

I had a fucking good-old-fashioned, bona
fide, hand-to-God *LOVE TRIANGLE* on my
hands!
It's such an *old* fucking story!

I got back in the car,
sat there in the driver's seat,
there in the strip mall parking lot,
squinted from the sun as I lit a cigarette,
blew smoke hard up toward the ceiling,

and wondered what would happen.

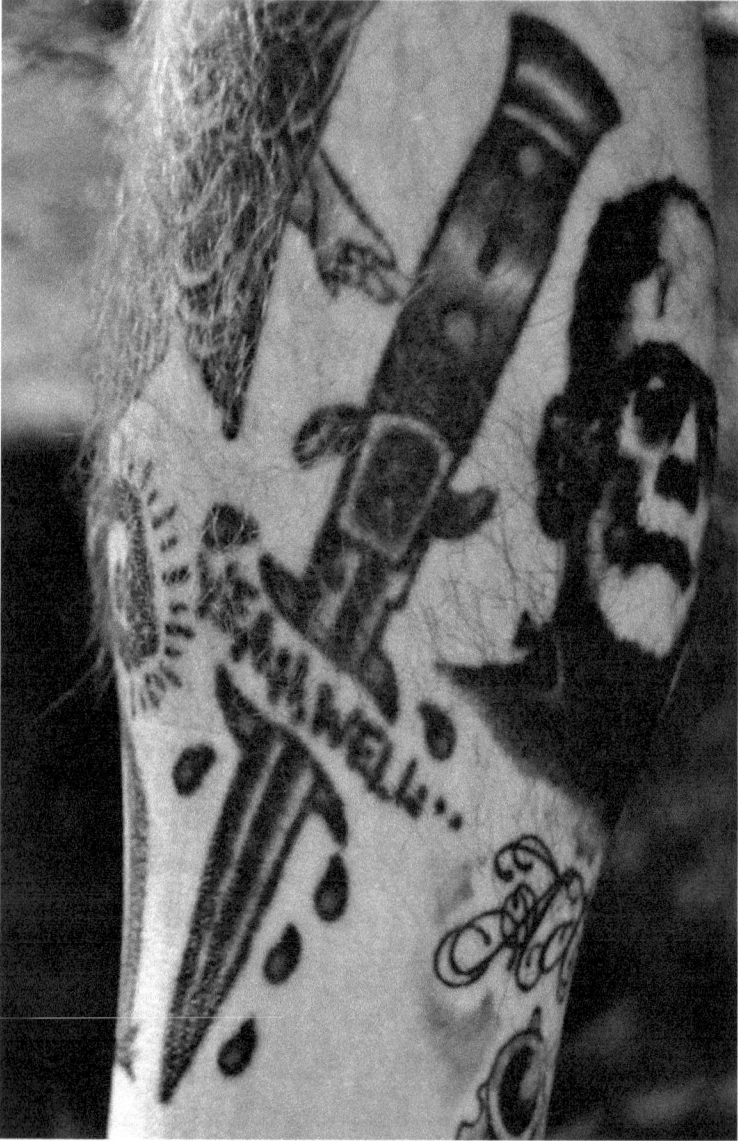

Photo: Brett Reed

Underground poet Joel Landmine was born and raised in the San Francisco Bay Area. He got his start at the now-defunct *Tenderloin Reading Series,* and has been a mainstay of the *Anger Management & Revenge* and *Bitchez Brew* reading series. He has been a featured reader at San Francisco's Litquake festival five years running, and Oakland's Beast Crawl festival, as well as countless other Bay Area reading series. He has begrudgingly survived several near-death experiences. He lives with his cat in Oakland, CA. This is his first collection of poetry.

More About The Book And The Author

"The stories [he] told me… were remarkable in the characters' relentless persistence in unrewarding and depressing activities."
–A Psychiatrist

"Each one of these poems is a broken tooth you can't stop flicking with your tongue."
–Bucky Sinister, Poet, Author, Comedian, Strongman

"[His] are the only poems I would pay money for besides Walt Whitman's."
–Nate Lane, Gardener

"A naked nerve on the edge of a blade, this book. Every line is a cut. Landmine shocks you to life. Catharsis, Beast Generation Style, at its best."
–Zarina Zabrisky, Author of *Iron* and *We, Monsters*

"It's pretty good."
–Jon Nelson, Retired Bus Driver

"I crawled over Joel Landmine's brain laying in the gutter and Albert Fish spilled out posing as Sigmund Freud spitting on pigeons and screaming that he fucking hated Morrissey.… and I knew I was in love."
–Sammytown, Singer, *Fang*

"What the HELL is this?!"
-some angry old hippie at a reading

"Reading Joel Landmine is like receiving a kidney punch while having sex. His work evokes visceral emotion combined with a twisted sense of humor that comments on the human condition."
-Tony DuShane, Author of *Confessions of a Teenage Jesus Jerk,* Columnist for the *San Francisco Chronicle*

"Joel Landmine's gift isn't his ability to mine out shining little nuggets of life's absurdity as it exists between the haves and the have-nots drawn from the mass of humanity (which he also does) but the fact that his own authentic voice is so aware of these shifting dynamics. His voice is that of both the stooge and the fool, in the deepest sense of those archetypes. And he knows it. This is all a fancy way of saying he is a storyteller who deals only in brutal honesty; the best kind of storytelling."
-Paul Corman Roberts, Writer, Editor of *Full of Crow*

"Nothing like being horny and sad all at the same time."
-Pamela Chao, Bartender

"[His] book is that familiar wise-crackin' old so-n-so with a heart of beaten gold.

There, now it's a quote."
-SB Stokes, Poet, Author of *A History of Broken Love Things*

Other Punk Hostage Press Titles

Forthcoming from Punk Hostage Press

When I Was A Dynamiter (2014) by Lee Quarnstrom

Dead Lions (2014) by A.D. Winans

Where The Road Leads You (2014) by Diana Rose

Disgraceland (2014) by Iris Berry & Pleasant Gehamn

Long Winded Tales of a Low Plains Drifter (2014) by A. Razor

Boulevard of Spoken Dreams (2014) by Iris Berry

Dangerous Intersections (2014) by Annette Cruz

Driving All of the Horses at Once (2014)
by Richard Modiano

The Red Hook Giraffe (2014)
by James Anthony Tropeano III

Dreams Gone Mad with Hope (2014) by S.A. Griffin

In The Shadow of the Hollywood Sign (2014) by Iris Berry

Puro Purismo (2014) by A. Razor

Appetite for Dysfunction (2014) by Vicky Hamilton